W9-AGQ-158

the **offense**. The second team is called the **defense**. The defense is trying to stop the offense from scoring points. The offense and defense do not stay the same throughout the game. Each team takes turns trying to score points or stopping the other team from doing so. Much of football has to do with numbers. You can use your math skills to help you learn more about this action-packed sport!

Figure It Out!

Counting the number of players on the field is important. If your team has too few players, your **opponent** could beat you. If your team has too many players, your team could get a **penalty**. Count how many players the red team has on the field below. How many blue players are there? Does each team have 11 players? How many players need to leave the field?

(See page 22 for the answers.)

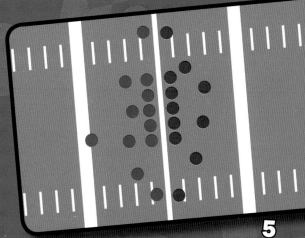

Get Out Your Measuring Tape!

A football field is 100 yards long. There is a bold white line down the middle called the 50-yard line. This line divides the field in half. Each team defends their own half of the field. There is a goal line at the end of each half. Each team tries to cross the other team's goal line.

Here the New Orleans Saints and the Indianapolis Colts line up at the 25-yard line before a play.

It's a Fact!

Football fields are measured in yards. One yard is equal to 3 feet (1 m).

To help players understand where they are on the field, there are white lines every 5 yards. Every other line, or each 10-yard line, is labeled with a number.

The field is 160 feet (49 m) wide. There are white stripes, called sidelines, that clearly mark the sides of the field. The players must remain inside the sidelines to continue playing the game.

Figure It Out!

The end zone is the space between the goal line and the **goalposts**. There are two end zones, one at each end of the field. Each end zone is 10 yards long. How far is the distance between the 50-yard line and one of the goalposts? How long is the whole field, including the end zones?

(See page 22 for the answers.)

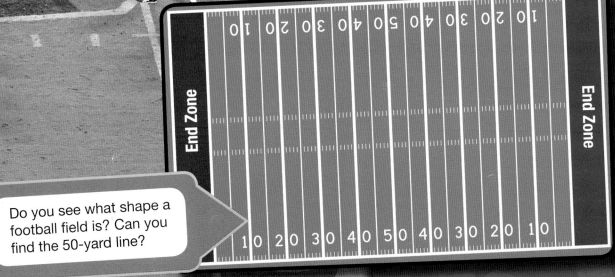

Do you see what shape a football field is? Can you find the 50-yard line?

Point Math

The object of football is to score points and beat the other team. There are several ways the offense can score points. If a player kicks the ball through the goalposts, he has scored a field goal. A field goal is worth three points. If a player runs with the football past the goal line or catches the ball in the end zone, the offensive team scores a touchdown.

It's a Fact!

The defensive team can score points, too! When the defensive team tackles the offensive team in their end zone, the defensive team wins two points. This is called a safety.

A touchdown is worth six points. After a team scores a touchdown, it has a second chance to score more points. The offensive team can kick the ball through the goalposts for one more point. It could also try for a two-point conversion instead. This means a player runs the ball past the goal line for two more points.

Here Tracy Porter of the Saints is scoring a touchdown. That is six points for the Saints!

Figure It Out!

The Cincinnati Bengals are playing the Baltimore Ravens. The Ravens score a touchdown, plus they get the extra point. The Bengals kick a field goal then score a touchdown. The Bengals also kick the ball for an extra point. Next, the Ravens score a safety, and the Bengals score two field goals in a row. What is the score of the game? Make a chart to help you keep track of the points scored by each side.

(See page 22 for the answers.)

Moving the Ball

When the offensive team has the football, it gets four chances to move the football farther down the field. These four chances are called downs. If the offense can move the football at least 10 yards down the field, then the team gets another first down and gets four

Here the referee is measuring to see if the team made a first down. The football needs to be at or beyond the place where the orange marker reaches.

more chances. It uses these downs to try to move 10 more yards toward the other team's end zone.

Sometimes the offense may have used up three downs and is not sure it can cover the yards that are left to make a new first down. In this case, the team may decide to punt. This means the offense kicks the ball to the defensive team. The hope is that the other team will catch or stop the ball at a place that is farther away from scoring points.

Dave Moore of the Tampa Bay Buccaneers makes a first down here.

Figure It Out!

The Seattle Seahawks have the ball. They are the offense and it is first down. They move 6 yards during the first play. On their second play, they move another 6 yards. Then the Seahawks move 4 yards on their third play. What down is it now?

Hint: Remember that the team needs to move the ball 10 yards to get back to a first down.

(See page 22 for the answers.)

Time!

Every football game has four time segments called quarters. A quarter means that it is a quarter, or fourth, of the total length of the game. Four quarters equal one game, just as four quarters equal $1.

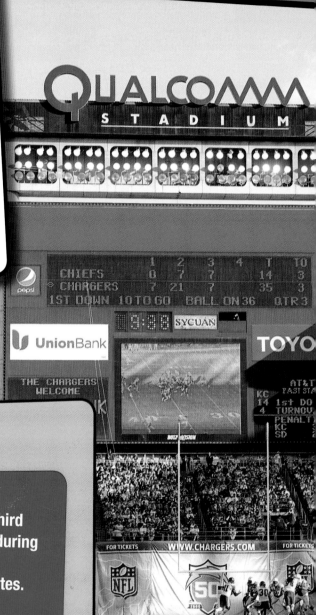

It's a Fact!

Between the second and third quarters, the players rest during a break called halftime. It generally lasts for 12 minutes.

In the National Football **League** (NFL), a **professional** football league, each quarter is 15 minutes long. A whole game is 60 minutes long, or 1 hour. How can you figure this out on your own? Write down the facts you know as a math **equation**:

4 quarters x 15 minutes = 60 minutes.

Another way to write this is:

15 minutes + 15 minutes + 15 minutes + 15 minutes = 60 minutes.

Figure It Out!

1) In a high-school game, each quarter is 12 minutes long. How long is the game?
2) If a quarter in your town's football league lasts for 8 minutes, how long is the game?

(See page 22 for the answers.)

Football stadiums have scoreboards to help fans keep track of the game. You can see how much time is left in the quarter at the center of this board.

Penalties

There are many rules in football. These rules help keep players from being hurt. They also **ensure** a fair game. Penalties are given out when players break the rules.

For example, there is an offensive player called a

Hanging on to a player's shirt and pushing him like this are penalties. Do you see the yellow flag?

quarterback, who is the leader of his team. The quarterback gets to say when a football play begins. No player can cross the **line of scrimmage** until the quarterback says so. This happens when he tells a teammate to **hike** the ball to him. If a player moves over the line before this, that player's team is penalized by having to give the other team some yards. There are many other ways to get penalties, too.

Figure It Out!

If a penalty is called on the defense, the offense can move closer to the defense's end zone. Say the offensive team starts a play on their 45-yard line, but the defense is called for a 5-yard penalty. Where does the offense start the next play?

(See page 22 for the answers.)

Referees throw yellow flags on the field when they call players for penalties.

The Standings

Most football teams are in a league. The teams are ranked to show which team is best, which team is second best, and so on.

These rankings are called the standings. The standings are organized by each team's

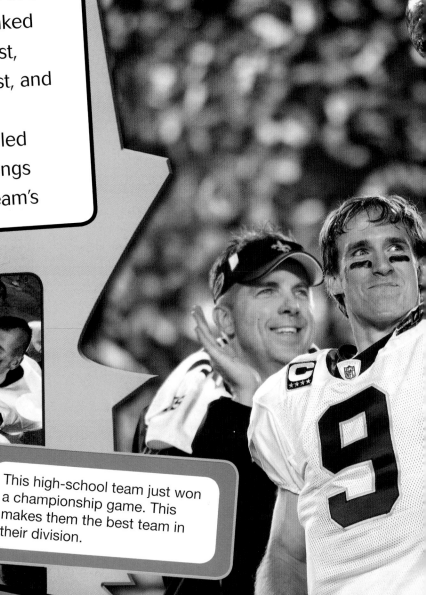

This high-school team just won a championship game. This makes them the best team in their division.

winning percentage. A team's winning percentage is found by dividing the number of wins a team has by the number of games the team has played. The team with the highest winning percentage is in first place. If the Raiders have won three games and lost two, they have played five games. Their winning percentage is $3 \div 5 = .600$. Winning percentages are rounded to three decimal places.

1) What is the winning percentage for Team A if it has played seven games and won four of them?
2) What is the winning average for Team B if it has played six games and won five?
3) Which team has a higher standing?

(See page 22 for the answers.)

Quarterback Drew Brees of the New Orleans Saints holds up the trophy the team received for winning the Super Bowl in 2010.

It's a Fact!

"Percent" means "parts per hundred." An average is a middle value of a set of numbers. A team's winning percentage is really the average number of wins it has in a set of games. "Winning average" may sound funny, but it better describes the math!

What Are Stats?

You may have heard people talk about a player's or team's stats before. "Stats" is short for "statistics." Statistics is the study of groups of numbers. People look at many numbers to help them **evaluate** how good a team or player is. Winning percentage is one example of a statistic.

Many statistics in football count things. For example, counting how many yards a team

Here are some stats from several of Peyton Manning's best seasons:

Season	Team	Touchdowns	Interceptions	Yards	Passer Rating
2009	Colts	33	16	4,500	99.9
2006	Colts	31	9	4,397	101.0
2005	Colts	28	10	3,747	104.1
2004	Colts	49	10	4.557	121.1*

* This is the highest passer rating in a season for any quarterback in history.

gained during a game or in a **season** helps us understand how good an offense is.

There are many harder statistics, too. One example is the quarterback rating. The quarterback rating looks at how successful a quarterback is at doing many parts of his job.

There are statistics for every player on the football field. One statistic for punters is the average number of yards they kick the ball. Charlie is a punter. He punts the ball 30 yards on the first kick, 32 yards on the second, and 34 yards on the third. How can you figure out the average number of yards Charlie punts the ball?

A) 30 + 32 + 34 = 96
B) (30 + 32 + 34) ÷ 3 = 32
C) 30 x 32 x 34 = 32,640

(See page 22 for the answers.)

Peyton Manning has great stats every year.

May the Best Team . . . Lose?

Statistics are important, but they do not mean everything. A team can have better statistics than its opponent yet still lose a game. That is what makes each football game so exciting.

A famous example happened in **Super Bowl** XXXVI. In the 2002 championship game, the Saint Louis Rams played the New England Patriots.

The Rams offense had moved the ball 427 yards. The Patriots had gained only 267 yards. The Rams had 26 first downs, while the Patriots had 15. This means the Rams had many more chances to score. The Patriots won, though, by a score of 20–17. The Rams had better stats, but the Patriots won because points scored is the most important statistic of all!

The chart below shows the two teams that have played in each of the last five Super Bowls. Each team's total offensive yards are listed along with the number of points it scored. What percentage of Super Bowl winners have had fewer offensive yards than their opponents? Are you surprised?

Hint: Percentage = (Games you are looking for ÷ Total games) x 100

Season	Away Team	Away Team Yards	Away Team Points	Home Team	Home Team Yards	Home Team Points	Winner
2010	New Orleans	332	31	Indianapolis	432	17	New Orleans
2009	Pittsburgh	292	27	Arizona	407	17	Pittsburgh
2008	New England	274	14	NY Giants	338	17	NY Giants
2007	Indianapolis	430	29	Chicago	265	17	Indianapolis
2006	Seattle	370	10	Pittsburgh	322	21	Pittsburgh

(See page 22 for the answers.)

Marshall Faulk of the Rams is trying to score a touchdown against the Patriots during the 2002 Super Bowl here.

Page 5: The red team has 11 players on the field. The blue team has 12 players on the field. 12 − 11= 1 player who must leave the field.

Page 7: 50 yards + 10 yards = 60 yards. The whole field = 2 x 60 yards = 50 + 50 +10 +10 = 120 yards.

Page 9:

	Ravens	Bengals
Ravens score a touchdown and one extra point.	7	0
Bengals kick a field goal.	0	3
Bengals score a touchdown and one extra point	0	7
Ravens score a safety.	2	0
Bengals kick a field goal.	0	3
Bengals kick a field goal.	0	3
TOTAL	9	16

Page 11: It is now second down. See the chart below to help you understand why.

Down	Yards Needed to Next First Down	Yards Gained in Play	Yards Needed After Play
1	10	6	4
2	4	6	They made it!
1	10	4	6

Page 13: A) 12 minutes x 4 = 48 minutes   B) 8 minutes x 4 = 32 minutes

Page 15: The offense begins the play again on the 50-yard line: 45 yards + 5 yards = 50 yards.

Page 17: 1) $4 \div 7 = .571$ 2) $5 \div 6 = .833$ 3) $.833 > .571$, so Team B has the higher standing.

Page 19: The answer is B): (30 yards + 32 yards + 34 yards) ÷ 3 = 32 yards. The average number of yards per punt is found by adding the yards that Charlie kicks the ball and dividing by the number of times he kicks the ball.

Page 21: $(3 \div 5)$ x 100= 60%

Glossary

defense (DEE-fents) When a team tries to stop the other team from scoring.

ensure (in-SHUHR) To make certain.

equation (ih-KWAY-zhun) A math statement that says that two different things are equal to each other.

evaluate (ih-VAL-yuh-wayt) To think about the importance of something.

goalposts (GOHL-pohsts) The uprights in the end zone where a kicker kicks the ball to score points in football.

hike (HYK) To quickly pass the ball.

league (LEEG) A group of teams that play one another.

line of scrimmage (LYN UV SKRIH-mij) The imaginary line between two football teams as they face each other to begin a new play.

offense (AH-fents) The team that tries to score points in a game.

opponent (uh-POH-nent) A team that plays against another.

organized (OR-guh-nyzd) Put in order or made rules.

penalty (PEH-nul-tee) Punishment for breaking a rule.

professional (pruh-FESH-nul) Someone who is paid for what he or she does.

season (SEE-zun) The group of games for a year.

Super Bowl (SOO-per BOHL) The championship game of the NFL.

Index

Web Sites

Due to the changing nature of Internet links, PowerKids Press has developed an online list of Web sites related to the subject of this book. This site is updated regularly. Please use this link to access the list:
www.powerkidslinks.com/sm/football/